Michael Creighton is a middle school teacher and library movement activist in New Delhi. This is his first book.

NEW DELHI LOVE SONGS

Michael Creighton

SPEAKING
TIGER

In association with the Jehangir Sabavala Foundation

SPEAKING TIGER PUBLISHING PVT. LTD
4381/4, Ansari Road, Daryaganj,
New Delhi-110002, India

Published by Speaking Tiger in hardback 2017

Copyright © Michael Creighton 2017

ISBN: 978-93-87164-51-2
eISBN: 978-93-86702-79-1

10 9 8 7 6 5 4 3 2 1

Typeset in Adobe Caslon Pro by SŪRYA, New Delhi
Printed at

All rights reserved.
No part of this publication may be reproduced,
transmitted, or stored in a retrieval system, in any form or
by any means, electronic, mechanical, photocopying,
recording or otherwise, without the prior
permission of the publisher.

This book is sold subject to the condition that it shall not,
by way of trade or otherwise, be lent, resold, hired out,
or otherwise circulated, without the publisher's
prior consent, in any form of binding or cover
other than that in which it is published.

*To my mother and father,
Susan Creighton and Michael Creighton*

CONTENTS

NEW DELHI LOVE SONGS

New Delhi Love Song	3
In the Early Days of the BRT	4
South Delhi Roadside, 8 a.m.	6
Cheap Bouquet	8
South Delhi Jungle Park	11
Tremor	12
Offering	13
Ode to Guava	14
Buzz	16
Next Life	17
To Bhagwan Kumar on the Occasion of His Daughter's Wedding	20
South Delhi Roadside, 9 p.m.	22
Meeting	23
Wish	25

ON THE BADARPUR BORDER

On the Badarpur Border	29
On the Rajdhani Express	32
Slowing	33
Bend	34
What the Rubber Farmer Said	36
Sacrament	37
Apologies to the Shakarkandiwala	38
Scattered	39
May Lychees	40

The Old Woman in Front of the Petrol Pump	41
Clover	42
Thin	43
Fulcrum	45
100 Feet down and Dry	46
Scent	48
Elegy	50
Breaking News	51

CIRCLE

Circle	55
Hinge	56
Father	57
Stopped	60
Station	62
The Last Time This Happened	63
To Shakti on the Eighth Anniversary of Her Death	65
Stirring	67
Lighter	69

INTOXICATED

Intoxicated	73
Water and Smoke	74
Advice	76
Escaping Chirag Dilli	77
Divinations	79
Peon	81
Condensed	83
Front-page Photo	84
Sunday Shave	85
Source	87

GARHWAL

Northbound	91
Bend in the Road	92
Reach	93
Hold	94
Calling Home	95
Climb	96
Manager's Quarters	97
Gaze	99
Fork in the Road	100
Visitation	101
A Woman Feeds Goats on a Hillside	102
Stones	104
Swerve	105
How Many	106
Mochi	107
10-rupee Fix	108
Hail One Down	109
I Have Heard People in These Hills Are Honest	110
Mother	111
Brother	112
Sister	113
Feed the Snake	114
Confession	115
Baptism	117
An Old Woman	118
Garhwal Ghazal	119

Acknowledgements   121

NEW DELHI LOVE SONGS

New Delhi Love Song

Smog and dust mix with the air in New Delhi.
I buy jasmine for her hair in New Delhi.

People come from everywhere to this city;
all are welcomed with a stare in New Delhi.

The finest things in life don't come without danger—
eat the street food, if you dare, in New Delhi.

We push in line and fight all day for each rupee.
Who can say what's really fair in New Delhi?

There is nothing you can't find in our markets—
socks and dreams sell by the pair in New Delhi.

So many families on the street through the winter;
sometimes good men forget to care in New Delhi.

Friends ask, *Michael, why'd you leave your own country?*
I found jasmine for her here, in New Delhi.

In the Early Days of the BRT

I'll never forget that 522
we waved down on Khel Gaon,
just as it started to pour.

Seeing me in my soaked shirt
and you in your bright red dress,
blue scarf, wet sneakers—

the only woman on that bus—
the conductor gave us his seat,
and several men smiled

and stared through
the crooks of their arms.
But by Ring Road,

all eyes had turned outward:
in that September rain,
Delhi's lights shimmered

like your long glass earrings,
and a film of oil rose
to the top of the tarmac,

leaving the road
a pigeon-neck green.
At the Moolchand flyover,

the driver turned up the volume
and an old song blared
through the radio's tinny speakers:

*Today the weather is faithless,
there's a typhoon on the way—*
then the bus lane cleared,

and we all sped south watching
the stream of cars
barely moving below us.

South Delhi Roadside, 8 a.m.

She is lovely, I think, as she sits,
one hand draped lightly over the shoulder
of her breathless companion,
the other moving up and out,
as it punctuates the monologue
she is murmuring in his ear.
Even from here, I can see that fine lines
break and run from her eyes,
and banks of invasive grey
have taken root in her wild black curls.
(Later today, I will read that Sharon Stone
has proven older women can still be beautiful,
and I will think—was there ever any doubt?)
My God, this woman looks like a queen,
except she is sitting sideways, balanced,
on the back of an old, black bicycle.

The late April heat is already up,
and anyone looking would see
this man of hers is hard at it;
his pressed white shirt has come untucked
in the back, and the slick bare skin
at the top of his head is pearled with sweat.
I wonder if he ever finds himself wishing
he could trade the load he is pedalling

for a bottle of cold water,
or an FM radio.

Suddenly, the corners of her lips elevate slightly,
and, taking his right ear between her thumb
and forefinger, she tugs.
His head snaps back,
mouth opens wide,
and he laughs with such force
that even the dogs drowsing
in the dusty shade that lines this road
lift their heads and sing.

Cheap Bouquet

After this long winter,
I think you deserve something good,
like a stem of orange lilies
from the flower stand downstairs.
I'd make sure one bloom was fully open—
a tiny 10 a.m. sun;
one might reveal its colour and form,
while holding close to itself,
as you often do;
the remaining three
would be wrapped in green,
unopened gifts for the days to come.

It would have travelled by air
last night from Bangalore,
and then by three-wheeler
from the Ghaziabad flower market
even before schoolkids sprouted
on the side of the road,
but I'm sure I could get it for Rs 120,
which seems like a pretty good price
for something so beautiful
that has journeyed so far.

But couldn't I afford
a little something more?

How about a 30-rupee bunch
of spring larkspur,
with dozens of small blossoms
crowding the green,
like strings of amethyst earrings
in a costume-jewellery shop?
I hear they grow right here in Delhi,
on a flower farm next to the Yamuna—
we could go see them someday;
I'm sure they would be lovely
in the early morning light—
or just before dark,
under a dust-bloated sun,
when their scent must mix
with the dead river's stench.

It's hard to be original
with a bunch of cheap flowers.
Still, the guys at the stand
are pretty good, and I think
at this distance, in this light,
yours might suggest something pleasant:
a pair of bright kites
rising out of a forest draped
in ropes of the old Japanese
fishing floats that sometimes
still wash up on Oregon beaches—

or something simpler,
like a song,
or a prayer wrapped in yesterday's news
and offered with an open hand.

South Delhi Jungle Park

with Surya, age four

The beetle walks on its front legs,
back legs pushing a ball of dung across our path.
You complain the ants will bite you
if we don't keep moving.

Even the neon-necked peacock fails
to hold your attention;
there is grit between your toes,
a bothersome slipperiness in your
puddle-soaked sandals.

Only the tiny purple and brown
speckled egg on the path before us
stops your complaints. *It's beautiful,*
you say, *let's take it home and hatch it.*

I place the egg in my breast pocket,
knowing there are things
I'll never be able to explain to this little girl—
the hopelessness of a fallen egg,
the bright yellow stain that will appear
some hours later on my white shirt,
just above the place
I imagine my heart to be.

Tremor

Today, my students asked me if I'd felt
the tiny quake that rattled loose windows
in the city last night and what I'd been
doing at 9:30 when it happened.
I started to say, no, I hadn't noticed,
when I remembered that at 9:30
you'd emerged from your bath—
the lights were off, so you wouldn't be visible
to the men slapping out roti on the roof
of the market across the narrow lane
behind our flat—but as I studied you
from where I sat on the cool floor,
I measured in the angles of your limbs
and the length of your curves,
the same degree of grace and gravity
I had seen there the very first time
I saw you like this, in similar light,
a dozen years ago this spring.
And recalling how I felt last night
as you scolded my gaze—
your quick-lifted chin only half hiding
your smile—I turned to my students and said,
yes, I did feel a tremor,
now that you mention it.

Offering

Was it faith, or simply lust, my love,
that brought us to that hall of trust, my love?

Others demand prayers and burnt offerings.
What have you asked of me? Just my love.

Dense fog can warp the widest Delhi roads;
at times, I know, you must have cussed my love.

To prime old pumps, you need a patient hand—
recall that first night, how you rushed my love!

Last night I tasted salt and sandalwood;
at dawn, you kissed me, and I blushed my love.

You cry, 'Michael—the haze is thick, this year!'
Warm rains will come to clear the dust, my love.

Ode to Guava

I knew you first
by another name.
It was August,
and an old woman
seated on the footpath
in the central market
sliced bright green globes,
sprinkled them with dark powder,
and announced: 'amrood'.
So naïve I was in those days,
so easily thrilled by the idea
of you as forbidden.
That infatuation was fleeting—
what danger is there really
in dry powder and cut fruit?
But I never forgot the way
your sweetness
bore black salt and spice,
and how you returned
to me faithfully each August.
If I lived in Kochi,
I might sing for a banana;
for a mango, if I lived
in Chennai, or an apple,
if I still lived in Portland.

When my Grandfather
lived in Tampa, he sang
only orange,
but he told me once
that he'd loved you too,
as a young man during the war,
ashore and far from home.
I confess, I might love
only lychee, if I dwelled
on the cusp of May and June,
but I live here in Delhi,
and now, and I hold you
above all others: yellow
and soft, or green
and hard—salt or no salt—
your flesh, your seeds,
your skin, I leave nothing
behind save your stem.

Buzz

You were in my dreams again last night.
I was back in Oregon, sitting with the kids
on the side of a rural road. They were drawing
the red barn, and I was looking
for chickens and wheelbarrows.
My mother appeared and scolded
me for not joining in with the art project.
I said, Mom, the kids are having a fine time;
please just let me sit here
and finish this poem.
She shook her head
and I could hear her thinking,
they'll be grown before you know it,
Michael, it all happens so fast.
It was right then that your text buzzed
in my pocket. I didn't open it, though,
which was probably a good thing,
because when I woke,
I found my mother had been right:
the chickens and wheelbarrows
were right where I'd left them,
and the kids were already grown.

Next Life

Considering the piles of books
that jumble the floor by our bed,
I could almost imagine you happy as a postbox
on the corner of some crowded city street.
No doubt, you'd digest with relish
the scribbled stuff that passed through you—
but in the end, you'd be self-conscious,
standing alone all day, upright
and so brightly painted.

No, best that you, always incisive in this life,
return as something sharp—
a pair of kitchen scissors,
or a table saw with a diamond-tipped blade.
You wouldn't like your room in the dust-covered basement,
but there'd be plenty of other tools
down there to keep you company.
And I know you'd find it exhilarating
to whine and spin and bite your way
to the heart of every matter.

I have always loved the taste of shifting air,
and I feel certain eternal souls are not bound
by international borders;
I think I'd be well suited to life
as a New Delhi auto-rickshaw.

With neither the gravity of a car,
nor the grace and verve of a two-wheeler,
I'd nonetheless present a dashing enough picture
with my three wheels spinning below
and a roof of yellow rubberized canvas
pulled tautly over my light metal frame above.

In May and June, as my wheels ran slowly
over tarmac softened by the torrential
heat that falls from Delhi's skies,
my four-stroke engine would hum and purr,
'Thank God I'm metal and not man on a day like this!'
But I'd love cold December mornings best of all.
Then, I'd glide through ankle deep fog—
a skiff under sail, as I trolled the banks
of paved-over rivers,
searching for some ballast
to fill the empty seat inside me.

Or maybe if our love is as true as it seems,
we'll spend the Next Life
joined even more tightly than we are in this one.
You be a Hobart Mixer, and I'll be your bowl!
With your one-sixth horsepower motor
and attachments suited for slicing as well as blending,
you will still be capable of both analysis and synthesis.
Me, I've had enough deep thought and worry in this life;
I will be happiest as I spin, focused only on you above me,

as you, looking back down on me,
gently tickle my shiny belly
with your twirling wire brushes.

To Bhagwan Kumar on the Occasion of His Daughter's Wedding

In the years that follow,
who will remember
the grimy walls,
the flimsy plates,
or the sweat-stained shirts of the men
serving golgappe and chaat?

Even the strong smell of urine that crowded
the guests at the tables nearest
the toilets will fade,

leaving a score or so of the groom's men
dancing outside the wedding hall
to Bollywood tunes played by a full brass band.
The groom will arrive on a white horse,
a fat garland of 10-rupee notes
strung round his neck,
fireworks hanging above him in the sky
like burst pomegranates.

And you will be there, taking his hand
and leading him into the photo:
he and your daughter,
flanked on one side by his parents,
on the other by your wife

and by you, in your brand new suit,
chin lifted, back straight,
showing no sign of your smile.

South Delhi Roadside, 9 p.m.

As you sell your last
half-melted mango popsicle
and start to push
your cart home,

you think that by now
the ice must be melting
high in Himachal.

Perhaps she is banking
the fire early tonight. Perhaps
she is stepping out
to piss.

Perhaps she is watching
winter wheat ripen
in moonlight.

Meeting

What feeds this long ribbon:
clean rain,
crooked rows of brick and tarp,
the ancient, unruled quarters—
Chiragh Dilli, Kotla Gaon,
Shahpur Jat.
A thin flow at Sainik Farms,
by Sheikh Sarai,
it is fat and ripe.

Before dawn, shapes squat
on these banks; by noon, pigs
splash and root in the shallows.
Above, boys sort trash
and throw stones at dogs;
downstream, strong men
strip off their shirts
and bathe in a leaky
main's spray.

In today's grimy sky,
the evening sun glows
like an electric tangerine,
and wood smoke from campfires
covers the scent
of swamp gas and sewer.

Sometime tonight,
this slow current will join
something larger, somewhere

an old woman will sing an old song:
After so long, the moonlit night has come,
after so long, this meeting.

Wish

I am a man of faith; I never doubt you.
And when I think of need, I think about you.

You cry when sparrows fall, but you defeat me;
there is no army standing that could rout you.

Some nights, I wander, seeking untouched places.
You taste of salt and jasmine as I scout you.

I'm just a fountain; you're the spring that feeds me.
I breathe your wetness in and then I spout you.

Named for the archangel, but still I've fallen.
Salvation's just a prayer, a wish, without you.

ON THE BADARPUR BORDER

On the Badarpur Border

We take the Violet Line as far south
as it will carry us and start walking
into the borderlands. You tell me

you are looking for a language
with which to speak of this place
and others like it, but I have little to offer:

I'm not even sure what state we are in now,
and when you ask, I can tell you neither
the name nor the source of the dark pool

that rests there between worn bricks
and hard ground; it hasn't rained for days,
so I suspect it is fed by one of the small drains

that run through the jumble of shacks
that line this road, but we're not close
enough to smell it, so I can't be sure.

There are mysteries in this land
between city and sprawl
that would take much digging

to uncover: the origin of the cluster
of well-built flats we passed through
just now, or how much of the green

and brown hillside near the railway tracks
is trash and how much is soil—
whether we should name it 'landfill'

or 'landscape'. Of course, there are things
I'm more confident of: I'd call that oxcart,
an 'oxcart', and that auto, an 'auto',

and from their lean and smiles,
I'd call the pair of straight-backed men
that just pedalled past us, 'friends'.

In the end, so much depends on us:
we'd agree that the rows of new and used
bicycle wheels hanging outside that shop

are 'cycle wheels', but while they remind me
of a cycle mechanic I once loved in Portland,
for you they will conjure something different,

and perhaps even more beautiful.
I don't ask you about the fine dust
that floats all around us, but to me

it tastes like grief and home,
and as for the smoke that hangs
between us now, it is a ritual,

but what I don't tell you is that for me,
it is also a prayer, like the point in the Mass
where the priest says,

*Pray, my brothers and sisters,
that our sacrifice may be acceptable.*

On the Rajdhani Express

with Akshay, age seven

Thirty hours south of New Delhi,
we roll past a jumble of tents.
You sit on my lap in the doorway—
one arm outstretched and waving.

We roll past a jumble of tents
where a boy outside sees you and races,
one arm outstretched and waving.
The sky smells of train smoke and grass

where a boy outside sees you and races
like a wave rushing south through the twilight.
The sky smells of train smoke and grass.
The air suddenly turns wet and heavy—

like a wave. Rushing south through the twilight,
you sit on my lap in the doorway;
the air suddenly turns wet and heavy,
thirty hours south of New Delhi.

Slowing

The train slows for a signal
just south of Shamgarh station—
the 6 a.m. air smells of grass seed,

diesel smoke, distant water.
Along the track, shapes squat
in the half-light; from beyond

the engine's rumble, sounds:
a temple bell, a rooster's cry,
the knock and crack

of steel on stone.
Farther on loom smokestacks,
brickyards, the outline of women

hauling clay. At Kota Junction,
men get down to wash and spit.
On the platform, a sleeping boy

turns toward his mother,
and a chaiwala sings
as he pours:

There is no way home.
This is the only way home.

Bend

Southbound on the Mangla Express

By the bend at Bina Junction,
we are twelve in a space
meant for eight, but outside

there is sun and a boy
spinning a tyre
through a field of dry grass

and goats. Ahead in a line,
straight-spined women
balance water, an old man

squats and smokes
in the shade of a bush.
Late in the night,

the smell of something dead
slips through the train car's
open windows:

I dream of wide roads,
wheat fields, my father's white
hair, and the bend

in his back. Before dawn,
I wake, weighed down
by dried sweat and distance;

in Igatpuri station,
the women selling jamun
are silent,

but the chaiwala sings
in the day. Hours later,
just north of Goa,

we come out of a turn,
into a driving rain.
Cool at last, with only

one night to go,
we share cut cucumbers
and talk of home, heat,

and unexpected things.

What the Rubber Farmer Said

May 2004, Kottayam District, Kerala

Sit and drink your coffee—
when it rains like this, what else can we do?
See there—how I gather the water
that runs in crooked torrents from my roof?
My neighbours called me a fool,
but dented buckets and pans
have kept my well full, even when
those owned by this district's many fools
ran dry.

You can smell that, can't you?
I, for one, could not have borne this life
if I had not found beauty buried in the stench
of raw sheets of latex.

Yes, of course I pray.
For sixty years, I have given thanks
for my wife and six daughters.
And I praise God daily
for the thousand shades of green
that collide in these hills—and for
my neighbour's rice paddy field, where,
mixed with the sun's own yellow,
they all somehow settle,
calm and faintly glowing.

Sacrament

A short kilometre south
of Chemmalamattom's
Twelve Apostles' Church,
Sunil Thomas gazes
out the toddy shop's narrow window
towards a pile of spent rubber
trees stacked in the lot
across the road:

it's time to make a deposit
in the State Bank of India.
His father always said
a lucky man outlives his trees,
so save for the day when
yours no longer give milk.

The old man was right about that,
he says. But just as important
is to praise God daily
for the gentle burn of fried fish
and palm wine—
and for the tug and crack of rice
drying on an open hand.

Apologies to the Shakarkandiwala

Nestled in spent coals,
in a clay bowl that sits in a box on the back
of the Atlas cycle he is pushing through this market,
is all that remains of his day's work:
a single, once-warm sweet potato.

Since morning, he has peeled and sliced and sprinkled
dozens of these with lemon and spices,
and now, with less than an hour to go
before dark, I see him lean hard
on his handlebars.

I know what it would take to send this man home early:
one half-plate for me and one for the kid
picking through the trash bin on the corner just ahead.
But today I can't find the stomach
for cold shakarkandi. And now

he is swinging himself up
onto his cycle, wobbling
on his way to the next market;
and now he is calling: *shakar—*
shakarkandi!

Scattered

A load of bound-grass brooms
has flown off the back of his bicycle

and scattered,
like so many stalks of cut wheat.

Now he is squat-walking sideways, gathering,
just as he would back home in Himachal,

where there are no horns or hot tarmac,
and lungs fill with wind and sky.

May Lychees

Tito Marg, Delhi

His fruit cart stands squeezed
between steel construction barriers
on a road clogged with air bakes,
car horns and bicycle bells.
Tonight he sells mangoes, cherries
and the first lychees of the season.

A woman gets out of her car to scold him
for his high prices and for the bad cherries
hidden in the bottom of his boxes.
He protests, *no madam, they are all good,*
but drops his price from 100 to 80.
She cannot agree to anything more than 70
and leaves, shaking her head.

I buy a half-kilo of his lychees,
take them home and eat them for dinner.
The skins of some are grey, and some are red,
and all are covered with tiny bumps.
Inside, every fruit is sweet.

The Old Woman in Front of the Petrol Pump

Each night for a week
you've slept
on the narrow strip

that divides this petrol pump
from the main road's rush.
Wrapped in a wool shawl,

you squat or lie all day
on hard pavement,
never venture far

from this spot,
as if you were waiting
to meet an old friend,

or securing yourself a place
at the head of an unformed queue.

Clover

A week later, the bee man
returned with the remains
of another unwanted hive:
a few slabs of wax,
a plastic bag of honey,
and a dozen or so bees
which trailed him like smoke
from an old motorbike.
I bought 10 kilos last week—
I cannot take more, I said softly,
but he refused to listen and followed
me into the kitchen, pleading.
The shirt he wore was frayed,
his arms were hard and thin;
he smelled like sweat and soil
mixed with clover, sun and wind.
He stood there, jaw clenching,
until I laid my hands on his shoulders
and walked him from the house,
saying through a thin smile:
It is regrettable, brother,
but why should anger come
from something so sweet?

Thin

When the monsoon arrives,
they turn traffic barriers
into a line of open-faced dwellings,
each with a raised floor,
roof, and three walls—
a steel village, suddenly sprung
from the roadside mud,
as yellow and bright
as a row of spring tulips.

Farther south, we pick our way
through families of labourers
who sleep outside on sidewalk stones
they laid last week.
One thin boy lies
between his brother and sister—
like my middle son,
he sleeps with his left knee raised;
his right arm shields his face
from moonlight and the buzz
of streetlamps.

Next morning in my kitchen,
the screen-scattered sunlight is thin—
like the scratch of the sweeper's

stick broom on cement
and the shell of the egg that cracks
too soon in my hurried hand.

Fulcrum

In thick July rain,
three bare-chested boys
swing soaked shirts as they run.
Ahead, there is sun,
behind, more black clouds,
and a bike rushing
over wet road.

Then in the time
it takes a branch
to bend and crack in the wind,
the bike's rear tyre loses
touch with the tarmac,
making its front wheel
a fulcrum,
its rider a flailing dart—

and I remember a ripe mango
that once landed in front of our house.
I followed my son
to where it lay,
and he took my hand
as we watched
nervous flies and a line of ants
approach the ruined fruit.

100 Feet down and Dry

With Talib, age eight

To our right, a crumbling mosque
and a dirt road travelled by women
hauling water and wood;

to our left, peeling paint,
windows with bars,
high walls wreathed in sharp wire.

Eyes trained on the green gate
at the end of the alley,
you pull me through

to the wild park beyond.
Street sounds fade behind
a canopy of canary calls

as we follow the slim trail
that runs just behind
the locked shrine.

At the ruined well, I tell you:
there's been no water down there
for years. But you demand proof,

so we throw a small stone
through the iron grill,
turn our heads,

and count:
first comes a rush
of pigeon wings,

then the far-away crack
of our stone striking rock.
On the way home,

you study ants and kick pebbles,
while I watch puffs of dust
rise off the path we are walking.

Scent

Was it the bright-tailed bird
that had been hanging about
or a cat from the neighbour's balcony
that stilled the ten-day-old pair?
For two days, the parents stood guard
over their headless young;
you asked me to move them,
but I delayed: give them time;
they are small and will
dry out in this heat.
But pigeon squabs are big enough
to stink before they dry,
so on the evening of the second day,
I covered my face with a rag,
and shook them gently
into a plastic bag. They were heavier
than I expected, and I could see
other small lives had already
taken hold in that feathered earth.

The plastic bag could not contain
the smell, so I placed them
in another bag and walked
through the colony towards
the jungle park where we'd once

buried a pet hamster. My friend,
I can tell you this: if you breathe
deeply enough, you will find
the gentle scent of loss
in every gust of summer wind.

Elegy

for Shakti Bhatt

Years from now,
we may smile and sigh at the sight
of a horribly misplaced comma
or a ball badly thrown
by a woman in shoes
the colour of sky,

but right now, all we can see
is this paper kite crashing,
smoke rising from a corn-seller's coals,

and beyond, that thing with feathers
hanging high in a mulberry tree,
spread wings brushing
leaves and blood-red fruit.

Breaking News

Five years after the Gujarat Riots

In front of the hidden camera,
they boast of their work that week:
the pig they killed

and hung from the roof of a mosque,
a pregnant woman
slit open,

the hundreds they hunted,
hacked, burned—
'We are not feeble rice eaters!'

Babu Bajrangi declares,
his hand shaking
like a dry leaf.

The week the story breaks,
the temperature falls
and street-side campfires haze the air,

though it's not yet November.
Men clump and murmur
in the market,

and the squirrel my son raised
with a dropper and soft fruit
walks away in the mouth of a cat.

CIRCLE

Circle

Chor Minar

They say that some king used to fill
the holes in this old tower
with the heads of his kingdom's thieves,
that the ghosts of the thieves' grieving widows
still circle the tower at nightfall,
even now, seven centuries later.

Each dawn brings new birdsong and light,
but there are some things we never forget:
a head on a spear high above us,
those who leave smiling,
and never come back.

Hinge

Eight years on, she still sees
the sheet-covered form of her daughter,

one foot exposed,
and lovely,

wheeling away through the hospital doors.
Some moments are fulcrums

on which a whole world swings:
heavy footsteps and then

the knock;
the hastily called meeting

where the director announces,
It is with great sadness that I say this.

Father

I didn't really know him,
but you were my friend,
so when the director

asked me to speak,
I felt obligated,
even though I knew

you would not be there.
I had no good stories to share,
so the night before,

I spread two dozen books
on the coffee table
and started to search

for something true to say.
Satchidanandan had one that nearly
worked, and Bishop and Kolatkar.

I almost settled on Stafford—
the one I sent you—
but in the end, it didn't fit:

it was really about *you*,
and the far, cold waves
you and the ones who hold

your hands are standing before now.
Finally, I opened a slim volume
by Li-Young Lee, and when I read

'Have You Prayed?' I could hold
neither my sorrow,
nor my love.

Of course it was my own father
I was loving at that moment,
and his father,

and the father I yearn to be—
and that seemed to be as honest
a feeling as I was capable of

at that dark hour.
I knew I'd have to practice,
but there was so little time for that,

so the next morning on a crowded train,
I held the book in my right hand,
leaned into the silver pole

and I mouthed it, over and over,
like a prayer. I was wearing my glasses,
and my head was down,

so no one would notice,
but as we entered INA station,
I felt a hand on my arm

and heard a schoolboy say,
'Uncle, take my seat now,
you sit down, please.'

Stopped

The sun was high and my cycle's rear tyre was flat. But it held the air I pumped in and I was running late, so I threw my bag on the back rack and decided to race the slow leak in to work. By the crematorium just north of Deer Park, I had to pump in more air. You can fill a slow leak, but then it always leaks faster; by Africa Avenue, I felt rubber touch rim. I remembered the time I'd patched a puncture on a Portland train—I'd hung the front wheel on the cycle rack, popped off the rear one, and sat on the floor, pulling tools from my bag. The thumbtack in the tyre had made it easy to find the hole, but I was out of practice, and as I wrestled with the tube I felt the gaze of a dozen early morning commuters on the back of my neck. No, it hadn't been very graceful, but later my favourite cycle mechanic Kim Fey had said, 'Wow, man, you patched it and still made your stop? That is too cool!' And so I flipped my cycle on the side of that wide South Delhi road, and I wished I could show Kim the trick I'd learned from the cycle mechanic who sits off Khel Gaon near Shahpur Jat, who'd taught me that you don't have to take off the wheel (who wants to take off the wheel, when you don't have breakaways?), you just slip out the tube, bit by bit, pump in some air, and hold it close to your face—if you are lucky, you feel it, like a breath on your cheek. And then I thought, of course Kim would have known that trick, but that wouldn't have stopped her from acting like it was some big deal…and then I felt it, the breath, and I patched the tube and took off down the road, relieved that the sun was hot so everyone would think it was just sweat running down my cheeks, and I felt so glad for cycle mechanics everywhere, but especially for Kim, and I wished I could tell her how sorry I was that I hadn't heard she was going until she was already gone, and how much I regretted never sending her any of the postcards I'd imagined sending to remind her that if she came to Delhi I'd show her things she'd never forget and how she'd joined the small chorus of voices that rattle around in my head when I feel lonely, tired, or stopped by something so wonderful it calls out to be shared.

Station

Beware: we dream the world askew, my friends;
simple signs are seldom true, my friends.

The old priest called the carpenter again:
'Why has the sky withheld its dew, my friend?'

I asked the missionary at my door,
'Why not convert yourself into my friend?'

When dust and ash press down on Delhi skies,
some nights I find my way home through my friends.

Beneath the smoke that cloaks Azadpur Station:
so much fruit for us to chew, my friends.

If I could lay my heart on market scales,
they'd show how much of me is you, my friend.

Once, you cried: 'Michael, where is the sun?'
Above this smoke, the sky is blue, my friend.

The Last Time This Happened

We were young, so when you told me
you had time between treatments
and wanted to go somewhere far,
we found a car and drove. In Vegas,
we did what young men do: ate and drank
cheap, lost money on games
we didn't understand.
Later, in a roadside Utah bar,
we watched the finals—
my team was playing the Jazz;
you threatened to tell the locals
I was a Portland boy. I pretended
to be afraid, but I can tell you now
the fear I felt that night had nothing
to do with the locals; you were always
the largest man in any room,
and I knew you'd never be able to quell
your stubbornness or your devotion.
I can't say for sure if we saw
the Grand Canyon at dawn,
but I do remember a campfire,
and the smell of burning sage;
flirting with those two women,
and later on the long drive west,
how the stars hung over us,

brighter than any stars anywhere
have any right to be.
In LA, I met your mother.
There were cracks in the path
outside her house, a bottle of vodka
hidden among her potted plants.
You told me you were ready to head
north then. Today when we talk
and you complain once again
about the clouds in BC,
I remind you that where I live now
smoke and ash hide the stars,
that I haven't seen them in months—
but when your voice cracks as you explain
how being alone is harder
than the nausea or the fear,
I have little to offer.

To Shakti on the Eighth Anniversary of Her Death

I didn't go to work on your anniversary this year. It was accidental, but it seemed right when I realized. Mridu and I spent the day searching for the Yamuna. It took us sixteen stops on the Metro and two three-wheelers to find it: on ground blessed by the feet of Guru Nanak. We met a boy standing ankle deep in the mouth of a small feeder stream. The river there was shallow and it stunk. The boy did not look up, but he told us he was searching for coins and that there was no path north along these banks. We headed back to the road. After a time, we turned east through a construction site. On a dusty path under a half-built highway overpass, we were greeted by a security guard who seemed to understand our quest: he didn't ask us to leave; he told us where we needed to go. We continued north to the point where clean water mixes with the dirtiest drain in Delhi, and then just a few metres further to the ghats where boys go to play after school. The river didn't smell there, but it was so shallow you could roll up your pants and wade across it. We didn't, but several people did. Three hundred metres further, we picked our way through the traffic clogging the narrow two-lane bridge that runs over the dam where the city pulls the water we drink. The edge of the road was adorned with garlands, plastic bags, and other broken offerings. North, through a gap in the wall, we saw deep water, the river as it should be. We didn't stay long, and Shakti, I confess I forgot to pray, but I did think of you then, and again later, further south, as we drank beer and ate tofu at a second-floor Tibetan joint. Through the window, we watched the wide, shallow waters, lined with small farms and trees, and at that distance, Shakti, even a dead river looks lovely.

Stirring

We threw open the windows
last week, and now

morning sweat sprouts
on the brows of city cyclists:

the calendar says spring,
but where I come from,

we'd call this summer,
and you know we have no word

for what comes next.
Give me a cool breeze,

a ceiling fan,
and a cold drink at dark.

Listen to the roads shake
under the rush of night trucks;

the lazy dogs are stirring now,
and the moon is high

and bright as any moon
where the air doesn't carry

the weight of so much smoke.
Let's go find something good,

my love. Let's walk until
we reach new ground.

Lighter

The May sun falls on Delhi
in torrents, softening tarmac,
and releasing road dust

from the weight of yesterday's rain.
Your flat is empty now
but for a few scattered

boxes and neat piles.
You say you have a stack
of clothes to burn,

and wonder if my lighter
would be adequate to the task.
After this long year,

your words sound equal
parts afterthought, anger,
and grief,

but I just nod; in this dry heat,
even a thin match
would put cotton to flame:

soon all that remains
is a pile of ash
and a pair of broken blisters

on the fingers of my right hand.

INTOXICATED

Intoxicated

Southbound on Tito Marg

Where this morning a broken
legged pigeon flailed,
this evening there are only crows

pecking at a pile of feathers
and bones. The roadwork
is done, but the tents remain.

Above, moths mob the streetlights;
from the right comes the squeak
and splash of wet cloth on pans;

from the left, engines and horns.
Yesterday on this road,
old trees bent in the wind,

and dust hid the midday sun.
On the footpath ahead,
a woman pats her child to sleep,

and a pair of white-haired men
pull smoke from a pipe.
In the distance, an old song blares:

My eyes are not dreaming;
this world is intoxicated.

Water and Smoke

In the sudden rain, there's no escape
from the dank press of men
beneath the paanwala's tarp.

Some smoke, some scowl,
one laughs as he shoots
red streams of betel-nut juice

into the flooded street.
Last night, I dreamed
I dropped off the edge

of the earth, into rough sea—
and now I see my reflection
in the window of a car

running slow through rushing water:
new lines, grey clumps spreading.
Across the street, the asphalt mixer

belches steam and soot
and the wind picks up,
throws rain across our shoes.

From a passing radio,
comes the high-pitched wail
of an old Bollywood show tune:

Tonight, a burning lamp
will turn to water and smoke—
10 rupees buys a single, then:

scratch, suck, glow,
and the easy brush
of shoulders and smoke.

Advice

Something is happening—
a hawker is hawking his wares, perhaps,
or a friend is announcing a feeling
of great weight.
Step back, look and listen:
you may hear a crow calling,
or see a dog drowsing on the side
of a dusty road. This one is short,
but there's always room for a simile:
straightforward, like a mirror hung slightly
askance; or unexpected, like a green guava
gone bad from the inside out.
Focus now, we're halfway there:
look hard at the hawker again,
or the friend,
and uncover some small surprise;
how his cycle wobbles
as he rides to the next market,
or a word or two she says
that can be understood
in more than one way,
like that green guava up there
or the dust that hangs over the road
running next to the lazy dog.

Escaping Chirag Dilli

Four boys grip the wooden sides
of the three-wheeled cycle-cart,
pushing it through the August heat.
A fifth sits in front, steering,
his legs too short
to reach the rusty pedals.
Already listing under its load
of water jugs and cans,
the cart lurches
when its front wheel catches
on a crack in the road.
As the others yelp and groan
against the weight,
the small one hurls himself
onto the handle bars
just in time to right the leaning load.
The older boys slap his back
and suck wet air, while he
raises his shaking right hand,
flies it in an arc above his head
like the cricket star he has seen
on the TV at the local milk stand.

Later, while the sinking sun
throws its last light over the long lip of the earth,
he will relive this moment

as he flies a two-rupee kite
made of thin paper and sticks.
With gentle tugs and pulls,
he will ease it through the sluggish damp
that clings to Chirag Dilli's ragged roofline
like a sweat-sodden shirt,
then higher, until it joins
the dozens of other scraps of colour
that have escaped to stir
in stronger air.

Divinations

Jantar Mantar Observatory, Delhi

It has been nearly three hundred years
since Maharaja Jai Singh II
built this colossal collection of arcs and lines—
this impossible children's toy—
to measure the present
and reckon the future
through careful observation
of starlight and shadow
on stone. Just outside,

a coconut-milk seller sits
on a wool blanket laid over
brown grass and dust.
To his left is a pile of green coconuts,
to his right, a long blade
and a bundle of drinking straws.
Above, lodged in the contours
of a massive tree,
are the remains of incense
from his morning prayers,
a tiny portrait of Lord Hanuman,
and several bright orange marigolds.

Today, I see the coconutwala's tiny son
climb onto his father's shoulders.

As his hands explore thick black hair,
he holds his face still,
less than an inch from his father's head,

just as I did when I was his age,
just as I imagine Jai Singh did,
as he looked for signs of his future
in tiny white flakes
and in the smell
of soap and oil and age.

Peon

Since his promotion to peon,
he is seldom sent from the windowless office.
What he misses most: the sky
and the vendors in the market below,

especially the one in the 85-rupee sale shop
who stands knee deep in his wares,
throwing shirts in the air
like a farmer using the wind
to sift threshed wheat.

The first time he tried, it fell—
but this time, he's mixed the mud right,
layered it just thick enough to attach
the piece of broken mirror to the wall
of the stairwell where he sleeps.

He delivers a dozen cups of tea twice a day,
collects signatures, copies and files papers—
but mostly he thinks of a mud wall
and another piece of broken mirror
twelve hours away by train,

or of the cinema hall where he goes
on the second Sunday of each month
with the boy who works two doors down.
When they slick back their hair in his mirror

and smile their film hero smiles,
he feels something inside him rise,
like the clothes the man throws in the market,
or his voice as it sings,
85, 85, every shirt, just 85!

Condensed

In the dusty dawn, it drips
From the slant-topped tent roof of the South Delhi taxi
    stand,
Where a dozen drivers sleep,
Cheek-to-foot and sweating,
Months and miles from their families
And feather-skied farms.

As it falls, it gives off a faint odour:
part diesel fuel,
part corn roasting on coals,
as smelled by men who have fallen asleep
recalling the taste of food
prepared by loving hands.

Front-page Photo

Two children exchange festive greetings after Eid prayers at Delhi's Feroz Shah Kotla

Waves of white caps
spill from the door of the crumbling mosque,
bathing the path of broken stones
that leads to the road beyond.

But two stand apart,
in sharp focus, embracing.
Their clothes are new:
his brown kurta two sizes too large, but crisp;
the orange in her salwar kameez glowing,
like her smile,
like the sun sweeping the smog from the sky
on this late October Eid morning.

Sunday Shave

Maybe it was the two
too many shots
of Old Monk last night,

or a virus,
or just that the heat
here has been rising

for weeks,
like the scent that shrouds
the footbridge over

the local drain
or the flies hovering
over the compost

bin out back,
but there's so little traction
in today that I hardly

notice myself shuffle
down to the market,
where Zafar lathers my face

with cool water and soap,
takes his long razor
and sweeps my skin clean

of three days of grey.
Looking in the mirror,
I hear my handyman

friend Martin proclaim,
a coat of paint is thrifty magic—
like a well-pressed shirt,

a hair cut,
or a steady-handed
Sunday shave.

Source

Smog lies heavy
on the late April sun;
heat rises from the tarmac—
like a cloud of flies,
like prayers.
What else is there to do
on a day like this?
Stand in the shade
and sip coconut juice,
consider the source of dust
that lies on the path ahead.

GARHWAL

Northbound

The three-wheelers change colour
at the border,

and tilled earth replaces tarmac.
A man rides an old cycle

over a rough path—
listen,

can you hear the rattle of fenders
and the ring of his bell

over the train's rumble and clatter?
He does not look up as we pass.

Bend in the Road

It is a long day's drive from the tea stand
to the northern seat,

but two hours will get you to the junction
where this river comes into her own.

Don't rush, says the tea man
as he fans a pile of flaming sticks;

the flavours take time to settle and blend.
On the charpai in the corner,

the trucker smiles and nods
as he gulps.

Reach

The shadows are growing fast,
when you pass him just where the path

enters the wide, shallow stream.
You're in no mood for anything cold,

but still you have to wonder
just how much ice cream is left

in the box neatly balanced and strapped
to the back of his old black bicycle.

The rushing snowmelt soothes
the sore muscles in your calves

but the stones underfoot are uneven,
and a cycle's a wobbly machine.

My friend, proud men seldom ask,
but it's not too late to turn back,

to reach out your hand and offer—
What a shame it would be, brother,

to waste something so soft and sweet
on waters as cold as these.

Hold

Today the tree roots and terraces
hold, but gravity rules this valley.

Build your home on hard rock
and make way for flowing water.

The road crew seldom rests.

Calling Home

I thought of you this morning;
even as the sun threw its pale light

over the ragged eastern hills,
I knew it was drowning

in your western sea.
From far below came the sound

of yesterday's rain on its way
towards something larger—

let's meet there someday,
among the salt and swells.

Climb

It is early when we cross the new footbridge
and get directions to the village
from a man leading a train of donkeys
loaded with sacks of cement. The path
is steep, but the air is unoccupied
by the city's dust, rot and burn.
At the gate, the headmistress
offers us tea. After twenty-five years
in a school even deeper in the hills,
she says this post is nice, and the bridge
has made life even better—
until last spring, there was just the ferry,
or the footbridge 5 kms north.
We discuss class size,
her two married daughters
and her husband, a doctor
in the next state over.
In the centre of the room,
a desk. Along the far wall,
an almari and a neatly made
bed. On the trail below,
a man and his donkeys,
on their way back up the hill.

Manager's Quarters

There are no rooms left,
but I'm alone, so I agree to stay

in the manager's quarters.
There is a flicker and buzz

in the fluorescent light,
and the plumbing vents

a mixture of ammonia and sulphur.
I know you'd hate it,

but the price is right,
the bedding is clean

and on the second day,
I unjam the valve to the geyser

and coax from it a bucket
of hot water for bathing.

That night I fall asleep thinking
of the cheap guesthouse

we stayed in that year: the look
on our daughter's face,

and the way she flapped
her arms as she described

the finger-sized insects
crawling on the bathroom wall.

Gaze

I dreamt of you last night,
and the long, thick viper you found

coiled next to one of the boulders
that litter this beach.

Has it really been a decade since
that afternoon? You said you felt its gaze

on the nape of your neck as you picked
your way back to us.

I see you now, shaking in slanted light,
the children behind you,

waving their arms and shouting
with fear and nervous delight.

Fork in the Road

I am missing you as we cross
the old footbridge

and approach the small shrine
to a solitary God.

His wife sits on the ridge above,
four hours up this trail.

If you were here, we'd visit her,
but today, I don't have the strength.

We meet a man going our way
who recites the history of his village

from founding to electrification.
We watch more TV now, he says,

but the paths are just as steep.
Where the trail splits, he stops

at a pile of stones. He says
a fork in the road is a good place

to pray. We turn around when the light
begins to fade. That night,

the pain in my heel returns. I dream
of leopards and lonely Gods.

Visitation

In the dark corner of the wall
just above the foot of my bed,

rests a spider half the size of my hand.
If you were here, I'd have to get up

and do something about it;
I wouldn't kill it—

superstition aside, imagine the stain—
but I think I could manage to trap it

with that dustbin and this journal—
oh my love,

they have come, suddenly young,
to this room! The big one,

all shouts and waving arms,
is crouching just behind me;

the little one has tucked his knees
under his chin and is studying his brother

out of the corner of his eye.
I reach for the dustbin, crying.

A Woman Feeds Goats on a Hillside

She is feeding the goats outside
her hillside home, when we meet the mother
of the boy with a broken back.

He'd been gathering firewood
high in a tree, five winters ago,
when he fell—

it happens every year in these hills.
Months later, a strong man found
him lying in this home, with bedsores

big enough to swallow a fist.
The man and his friends found a doctor
and carried the boy on a plank

down this trail. They took him by cab
to the city—what good is a wheelchair
in hills such as these? Later, I will meet

the boy-turned-man in Delhi. I will see
him dress himself and load his folding
wheelchair into an auto. He will post

videos from his smartphone and fly
to Bangalore to study computer science.
Every word I have written is true:

*broken back, bedsores, strong man,
smartphone—*

But five years could fill an ocean,
and elision's a conjuror's tool;
only this much I am sure of:

*a woman feeds goats on a hillside,
missing her faraway son.*

Stones

Is it the bed of jumbled rocks below,
the green and blue of the trees
and sky above,
or the shape of the space
between these hills
that's turned last week's snow
into the river that runs before us now?
Choose your stones carefully,
my son. We are changing
the face of something great.

Swerve

Before the first bird stirs,
northbound goods trucks sprinkle

the valley with horn blasts
and swerving light.

Once that summer,
when you were small,

we hitched a ride in the back
of one of those trucks;

we rattled and clutched
all the way down,

and we beat the evening
rain home.

How Many

leeches are hidden,
under your soaking
wet shirt?
Close your eyes,
and count to ten—
this will only
hurt for a
moment.

Mochi

In the last city
on a fickle grid,
why not get your hair cut
with pump-action clippers
and talk with the man
who spends his days
repairing torches
and shoes?

10-rupee Fix

It was bright and strong, with a black rubber case—
not some cheap local make.

And though it bounced, its bulb couldn't take
being dropped from a first-floor window.

The man on the footpath searched through his pile,
struggling to find a replacement.

Then he scratched his head, picked up a file
and put things right in a moment.

Hail One Down

There's always
room for one more
in the southbound
shared taxi. We've
just got ten seats,
but the two in the back
are large enough
to hold four.
Eighteen is as good
a number
as any other,
and everyone's
got a lap, no?

I Have Heard People in These Hills Are Honest

I.

That is what they say.
Not to worry—
no one on this trail
will rob you or fail
to loan you a torch
if you are ever
caught out after dark.
Just leave it below
at the home nearest
the footbridge.

II.

Thank you.
We are a long way
from the city
up here.

Mother

You were six, the day the cow herder's son
walked us up the hill to the pasture

where his family slept with their cattle
in their earthen-floored summer home.

Above, dense forest and sky;
below, the thin ragged ribbon—

that summer, the rains seldom
came before dark. We sat on the floor

as his mother fed us cauliflower
cooked over hot coals. Then came the pair

of tall steel cups filled with sour
buffalo milk: I loved you

for trying and for your relief
when I turned magician,

switching cups when no one was looking.

Brother

His mother said it had been cold,
so they'd tried warm oil and prayers

for days before they carried him down
the hill and caught a bus

into town, where the doctor said:
too late, you've come too late.

His family taught him how to speak
with face and waving hands:

simple feelings, actions, things;
places to go and leave.

He must be grown by now, but he
was twelve the year he walked

us past the temple to the school
high up there on that hill.

The doors were locked, the students gone,
he'd never been that close;

he peered through windows, studied desks
and did not want to leave.

You asked me: how would *longing* feel,
without a word to hold it?

Sister

Later, the bare-shelved shack,
the deaf brother, the sick cow's keening,

but right now, she's sitting next to a half-dug
field of potatoes, singing.

The melody is cousin to some minor key,
the words about Dehradun in the spring;

no clouds above—but in this breeze,
the taste of evening rain.

Feed the Snake

The sky is clear when a smiling girl
offers to lead us up the trail that connects

the road by the river to her village in the hills.
After an hour, she tells us to sit and rest.

'This pond and that tree are brothers,'
she says, 'and we leave milk on these banks

to feed the snake that lives here.'
My seven-year-old son shakes his head

and asks: 'But is the snake *real*?
Have you ever seen him?'

She shrugs:
'Why would we want to see him?'

In the valley below, yesterday's rain
flows towards the Bay of Bengal.

Confession

I will tell you how it happened,
as honestly and plainly as I am able.

On the third day, I was sitting like I did
each morning on one of those wide rocks

there by the river, sipping from a mug
of lukewarm coffee and talking

to the friends in my head about grief,
love and god. There was a breeze

on the back of my neck and the stars
were just starting to fade; the river

sounded just like she does today.
Faint light shone from behind

the eastern hills, and from the west
came stray horn blasts and headlights

from northbound goods trucks.
And then I thought:

Michael, why are you talking *about* her
and not *to* her?

So I put down my mug, stood and turned
from the chatter in my head,

and as I began my confession
I was entered and struck

by something so strong I can find
no good metaphor to wrap it in,

and I fell to my knees in the sand,
sobbing with sorrow and relief.

Baptism

At Laxman Bridge, a shower
of temple bells and traffic horns

crosses the river to reach us.
A diesel generator grumbles

to life on our right; behind us,
children are bathing.

The sun is bright and warm.

An Old Woman

After Kolatkar

There's a purpose behind our choosing
which stories we conjure or board,
like this train rushing south through the flatlands,

or the bus we pass heading north.
I'm only a common magician,
hiding balls under fast-moving cups:

you'll see what I choose to show you;
my tools are omission and flux.
The point's not the watching or telling,

but the struggle to see and to touch.
What's under the cup I'm not showing?
I can't say, but I'm sure of this much:

I have seen the temple walls fracture
and boulders break into sand.
I have heard the falling sky's clatter;

I'm reduced to small change in her hand.

Garhwal Ghazal

From the plains, dust clouds the view of these hills;
follow the trail of running blue to these hills.

In August rains, these slopes can slip anytime—
what parent doesn't sometimes rue these hills?

That bridge stood broken and unused for years;
the old quakes killed, but also grew these hills.

The truck mechanic fixes flats and rims;
he says no man or God can true these hills.

Yearly, pilgrims come to wander and pray.
Ill-mannered city boys run loose through these hills.

You ask, *Michael, what brings you back again?*
A faithless lover—I come to woo these hills.

Acknowledgements

Versions of these poems first appeared in the following publications:

Softblow: 'Meeting', 'Hold', 'Stones' and 'Bend'

Plume Poetry: 'On the Badarpur Border'

City: A Journal of South Asian Literature: 'Ode to Guava'

The Sunday Oregonian: 'South Delhi Roadside, 8 a.m.'

Verseweavers: 'Tremor'

Asian Age: 'Condensed'

Kaleidowhirl: 'What the Rubber Farmer Said' and 'South Delhi Jungle Park'

Ruminate: 'Apologies to the Shakarkandiwala'

Ego Magazine: 'South Delhi Roadside, 9 p.m.'

Tehelka: 'Breaking News'

Muse India: 'Front-page Photo', 'May Lychees', 'Next Life' and 'Divinations'

Prakriti Anthology: 'Escaping Chirag Dilli'

Orange Room Review: 'Scattered'

Wasafiri: 'On the Rajdhani Express' and 'Elegy'

Mint Lounge: 'New Delhi Love Song'

Pratilipi: 'Thin' and 'Fulcrum'

The Four Quarters Magazine: 'Wish', 'Circle', 'Slowing', '100 Feet down and Dry' and 'To Shakti on the Eighth Anniversary of Her Death'

Eclectica: 'Buzz'

The Sunflower Collective: 'Advice' and 'Water and Smoke'

The Poetry Mail: 'An Old Woman'

The Dhauli Review: 'Garhwal Ghazal', 'Source', 'Sunday Shave' and 'Peon'

I owe a great debt to Roger Weaver, my first poetry teacher.

Special thanks for those who read and commented on versions of this manuscript: Arun Sagar, John Morrison, Mridula Koshy, Souradeep Roy, Sujit Prasad, Terry Ofner, and most of all, Karthika Nair, whose insight and persistence were priceless.

I'm grateful for the members of The Community Library Project, the friends with whom I read poetry, and the Waters Poetry Forum for reminding me that reading and writing are collective acts of thinking.

Many thanks to Ravi Singh and Radhika Shenoy at Speaking Tiger, and to the Jehangir Sabavala Foundation for supporting this work.

ALSO IN SPEAKING TIGER POETRY

Nine: Poems
Anupama Raju

'Urgent and passionate, these poems circle age-old preoccupations of love and longing. This is perilous terrain where the danger of cliché lurks at every turn. However, without resorting to the easy distancing strategies of irony, the poet plunges into psychologically fraught zones of "poetry, perfidy and Pandora", ready to give voice to the vulnerability and confusion attendant on such an exploration. A quiet blend of authenticity and artistry sees her through, transforming familiar tropes of blood and longing, pain and death, into the "burnt letters" of warm, pulsating verse. Anupama Raju cuts close to the bone in this debut collection of poems.'—Arundhathi Subramaniam

ALSO IN SPEAKING TIGER POETRY

The Sand Libraries of Timbuktu: Poems
Rohinton Daruwala

'Rohinton Daruwala's poems unfold like a baramasa, an almanac of seasons and sensations, exquisite torments and explosions of delight. He essays a sensuous portraiture of place, invoking torrential monsoons, arid summers, railway bridges at night, libraries in deserts. [He] spells out a frank eroticism in the textures and flavours of fruit…at the same time, [he] is entangled in the hypermodern present. He gathers traces of the loved one from residues both material and digital… [He] maps the city, not only through the portraiture of human protagonists, but also through the micro-ecologies inhabited by butterflies and sparrows… In Daruwala's handling, the poem can be an oblique parable, a brief lamp of wisdom in the wind of distraction: light as breath, yet as essential.'—Ranjit Hoskote

www.ingramcontent.com/pod-product-compliance
Lightning Source LLC
Chambersburg PA
CBHW052052220426
43663CB00012B/2542